40 Days, 40 Prayers, 40 Words

40 Days, 40 Prayers, 40 Words

Lenten Reflections for Everyday Life

Bruce Reyes-Chow

WESTMINSTER
JOHN KNOX PRESS
LOUISVILLE · KENTUCKY

First edition
Published by Westminster John Knox Press
Louisville, Kentucky

15 16 17 18 19 20 21 22 23 24—10 9 8 7 6 5 4 3 2 1

Book design by James Satter
Cover design by Mark Abrams

Library of Congress Cataloging-in-Publication Data

Reyes-Chow, Bruce.
  40 days, 40 prayers, 40 words : Lenten reflections for everyday life / Bruce Reyes-Chow.
     pages cm
  ISBN 978-0-664-26189-4 (alk. paper)
1. Lent--Prayers and devotions. I. Title. II. Title: Forty days, forty prayers, forty words.
  BV85.R49 2015
  242'.34--dc23

                                                                    2015026174

Most Westminster John Knox Press books are available at special quantity discounts when purchased in bulk by corporations, organizations, and special-interest groups. For more information, please e-mail SpecialSales@wjkbooks.com.

This book is dedicated to my three daughters,
Evelyn, Abby, and Annie.

You remind me daily what it means
to be courageous, kind, and compassionate.

Thank you.

CONTENTS

ACKNOWLEDGMENTS

I don't take for granted the fact that I get to spend a good deal of my days writing, speaking, and traveling. While the travelin' life isn't as glamorous as some believe it to be, it's not an awful way to serve in ministry. I have no idea how long this season will last, but I do know it would not be possible if not for the support, encouragement, and patience of my family, friends, and community.

- **Fawn the dog**, because, let's be honest, you're everyone's favorite.
- **Robin**, for dealing with your spouse in all my frenzies, passions, and projects.
- **Annie, Abby, and Evelyn**, for making me laugh, for binge-watching cheesy shows, and for reminding me of the unexpected wonders and joys of life.
- **Lauren** (and the rest of my family, too many to name), for helping your brother with the creation of images, QR Codes, Instaprayers, and more.
- **Bridgett** and **Laura** from Presbyterian Publishing, who have been great colleagues over the years, offering support, prodding, and professionalism.
- **Jeff**, **Ellen**, **Luba**, and **Jenna**, for your pastoral leadership that continues to help me grow in my experience and expression of the holy.
- The community who covers me when I'm off gallivanting, I mean working, on important things: **Paul**, **Gigi**, **Mary**, **Kayvan**, **Rick**, **Kathi**, **Kara**, **Peter**, and **Stephanie**.
- And last but not least, **Philz Coffee in Noe Valley**, your creamy and dreamy Mint Mojito Iced Coffee drink has pretty much fueled every keystroke.

For all of you, I am grateful!

INTRODUCTION

Prayer is an interesting thing.

Some folks believe that prayer is a powerful act with the ability to heal, while others think it's an exercise in foolishness with the sole result being pacification. Some see prayer as a wish list for God populated by a list of items wanted or happenings hoped for. Some go through the motions every Sunday, while others maintain a fulfilling daily prayer life. Some pray with words and song, others through creation and movement, and others find stillness and silence as the prayer vehicle of choice. Some expect answers, and others pose questions. Some yell with confidence, and some whisper with fear. The meaning, practice, and intent of prayer are as wonderfully diverse as are the human beings who are doing the praying.

In the end, I don't believe there is a wrong or right way to pray. Prayer, in whatever form, is an ongoing conversation between humanity and God. Sometimes we hope for God to show up in particular ways, at other times we need to yell and wail at God, and at other times we simply need to let God know what's going on in our lives. Sometimes God's response is what we hope; at other times God answers in ways that are unexpected; and still at other times, God seems to remain silent. In the end, I trust that God does hear every prayer, and a significant part of our faith life is learning to listen for the many ways that God may respond.

There is, of course, the shadow side of prayer: prayer that is used to manipulate others; passive aggressiveness and judgmental attitudes couched as prayer; and prayer that is more about building up the one praying than about speaking with God. Like many folks, when prayer is used in any of these ways, especially in public worship or other public settings, I cringe and lift my own prayer that is usually something like, "Dear God, please don't let that last prayer work."

In the end, no matter how one prays or what one prays for, I trust that God is big enough to take it all in and handle both the good and the bad. While there are certainly times people need to be held accountable for the prayers that they may pray, the last thing that God needs is a bunch of us acting as prayer police trying to regulate theology and legislate content. Instead, I believe the best way to impact the culture and understanding of prayer is to offer prayers that reflect a theology and worldview that is in line with what we believe prayer should be.

Truth is, it is harder work to create new prayers than to deconstruct the prayers of others. I am convinced, however, that creating prayers that are contextually relevant and theologically consistent is a more effective way to share a theological perspective and to build relationships across the many differences of life and culture.

#40wordprayer

I offer *40 Days, 40 Prayers, 40 Words* as a contribution to the larger community. Not only do I hope to offer the written word, but I also hope to expand the ways in which we may connect. I have tried to create a space where liturgy, technology, and life converge by integrating social aspects to the process and product. All forty prayers are written using forty words so that they may be accessible in length and a reminder of the forty-day season. With these concise prayers, I hope that people will interact through *40 Days, 40 Prayers, 40 Words* in the following ways:

- Connect with others, through prayers I offer (or those written by others) with the hashtag #40wordprayer, across geographic locations, theological perspectives, and personal relationships.

- Allow people to easily share and connect on Twitter, Instaprayer, and my blog with Quick Read Codes (QR Codes) and links for each devotion.

- Provide graphics that can be used on most social networks as well as in paper bulletins or other hard copy resources.

- Read and share updated blog posts for each day that include downloadable images, prayers, reflections, and more.

- Offer resources for use of the Revised Common Lectionary (Year C) for Lenten reflections, worship planning, and/or daily prayer.

Hopefully, almost anyone can connect with *40 Days, 40 Prayers, 40 Words* regardless of theological perspective, technological capacity, or congregational context. Whether the convergence of technology and faith is your yesterday's news or if you are just dipping your toe into the waters of social media, I hope you will find a way to connect and engage with others around these prayers and reflections.

The Process

While *40 Days, 40 Prayers, 40 Words* is framed as a collection of Lenten prayers, my intention is that these prayers may be able to stand on their own. In order to give each prayer some autonomy and to avoid having each one be part of a bread-crumb trail leading to a particular liturgical destination, I approached the writing of the prayers with a particular process.

The first step was to choose the readings. From the daily lectionary readings for Year C, I randomly chose one reading for each day's reflection.[*] I generally rotated between a wisdom text, a Hebrew text, and a New Testament reading and used expansive language whenever possible. Although I think an important aspect of the lectionary is that it forces one to tackle texts that might otherwise be ignored, I did choose not to use texts if I got stuck or I just wasn't feeling it.

The next step was to write a prayer for each text. To do this I read through each of the aforementioned Scripture choices—*not in order and a little before and after the assigned text*—and wrote down the first few words and phrases that came to mind. After one pass through, I reread the Scriptures and solidified my theme choices. This allowed potential prayers and reflections to begin dancing together in my head. Then, I began a cycle for each of the forty prayers: writing the prayer, writing the reflection, and tweaking the prayer.

The final step was to create the graphics, Twitter updates, blog entries, Instapray posts, and corresponding Quick Read Codes (QR Codes).[†] This process was no easy task, but thanks to the help of Lauren Gibbs Beadle, you have what I believe are some cool interactive opportunities for *40 Days, 40 Prayers, 40 Words*.

How to Use #40wordprayer

Depending on what version of *40 Days, 40 Prayers, 40 Words* you are reading, the hard copy or the electronic version, you will access some of these components differently. The hard copy will have QR Codes or links that can be scanned with a

---

[*] Daily Readings from the Revised Common Lectionary can be found at www.commontexts.org.

[†] I used www.canva.com to create all images.

smartphone or tablet. The electronic version will have clickable links. Regardless of the version—*and thank you for purchasing either version*—you are invited and encouraged to use *40 Days, 40 Prayers, 40 Words* in the following ways.

See it!

This link will direct you to a blog post on my site [www .reyes-chow.com] where you will have access to each prayer. You can download an image for use in bulletins, newsletters, and social media; read part of a reflection; and find ways to buy or review the book. These resources are free of charge. I only ask that attribution is given whenever possible.

Tweet it!

Tweets have been created on through my twitter account [twitter.com/breyeschow] for each prayer that includes the prayer title, the graphic, and a few hashtags. This link will take you to that tweet so that you can respond to, mark as a favorite, or retweet any of the prayers.

Pray it!

As with Twitter, each prayer and the accompanying graphic has been posted on Instapray [www.instapray.com]. Accessible only through a smartphone or tablet app, this link will take you to the prayer where you can pray, re-pray, or comment on the prayer through your own Instapray account.

Let Us Pray

This has been a wonderful journey. The process of writing these prayers has reconnected me with some places in my own heart and mind that have been in need of care, challenging me to put into words my conversations with God—not an easy process but a fulfilling one.

With all these things in mind, I hope that you receive these prayers with the spirit and intent that they are offered: to be conversations with God about things that are important to me and I hope to others as well; to be theological statements informed by a reformed and justice-centered faith tradition; and to be words that will touch the souls of people at all stages of the journey of faith.

Thanks again for sharing your time and yourself with these prayers.

Let us pray.

on *COMMUNITY*

Ash Wednesday

Is not this the fast that I choose:
  to loose the bonds of injustice,
  to undo the thongs of the yoke,
to let the oppressed go free, and to break every yoke?
—Isaiah 58:6

WHEN I LIVE BELIEVING MY LIFE IS THE ONLY
LIFE THAT MATTERS,
GOD, REMIND ME THAT
THE FACES OF OTHERS REFLECT YOUR FACE,
THE STRUGGLES OF OTHERS BRING YOUR
LIBERATION TO MY LIFE,
AND THE KINDNESS OF OTHERS SPEAKS
YOUR GRACE INTO MY SOUL.
AMEN.

ON COMMUNITY
#40WORDPRAYER
@BREYESCHOW

When I live believing
my life is the only life that matters,
God, remind me that
the faces of others reflect your face,
the struggles of others bring your liberation to my life,
and the kindness of others speaks your grace into my soul.
Amen.

Every once in a while—OK, quite often—I have to remind myself that I am not the center of the universe. Yeah, yeah, I understand that I am a uniquely created child of God, but sometimes I can take this knowledge to the extreme and begin to think that life is all about me, and thus, in all things, the world should revolve around me.

Lent is one of those times where we can run the danger of reinforcing this idea: that our faith is ultimately about us and us alone, that the walk to the cross is to be taken in isolation, that blame for violence is to be laid at the feet of another, and that the resurrection is only a personal experience. Although certain aspects of Lent, and any Lenten discipline, require self-reflection and self-awareness, we must not enter that endeavor believing that it is only about our individual experiences. For we are reminded over and over and over again that the journey of life, the walk to the cross, and the experience of resurrection is a communal one—together we often turn on one another and away from God; and together we can experience forgiveness, repentance, and new life; and together we can be the best of who God intends.

So as we begin this journey, let's think about it as a collective of individuals on a journey, each discerning God's hopes and intentions for our personal lives while seeking freedom and justice for the larger community. Let's make this a time where it is about me—but it is also about you, about us, and ultimately all about God.

See it!	Tweet it!	Pray it!

on *COURAGE*

You who live in the shelter of the Most High,
who abide in the shadow of the Almighty,
will say to the LORD, "My refuge and my fortress;
my God, in whom I trust."

—Psalm 91:1–2

on courage

GOD, SOMETIMES, I AM
OVERWHELMED BY FEAR,
FEARFUL OF CHANGE,
FEARFUL OF OTHERS,
FEARFUL OF THE UNKNOWN.

IN THOSE TIMES, GRANT ME COURAGE,
A COURAGE NOT BORNE OUT OF FEAR,
BUT COURAGE THAT IS
GUIDED BY YOUR WISDOM,
GIFTED WITH YOUR PRESENCE,
AND GROUNDED IN YOUR CALLING.
AMEN.

#40wordprayer
@breyeschow

God, sometimes, I am overwhelmed by fear,
fearful of change, fearful of others, fearful of the unknown.
In those times, grant me courage,
a courage not borne out of fear, but courage that is
guided by your wisdom,
gifted with your presence,
and grounded in your calling.
Amen.

One of the most difficult aspects of engaging in self-reflection is that I might find something that I don't like about who I am, what I do, what I think, or why I do what I do. And even worse, I would then have to change my behaviors, my thinking, and my motivations. Who wants to do that?

I believe that most people are pretty good folks, and in our most honest times, we are able to acknowledge aspects of our behaviors and personalities that may need to change. At the same time, I also know that changing lifelong behaviors and ways of thinking, large or small, is not easy. Few of us can simply wake up in the morning and say, "Today, I am no longer going to judge people unfairly," or "Today, I am going to be compassionate toward all people," or "Today, I am not going to eat foods that I know are bad for me."

And yet, Lent is a time when we can explore changing, if even for a short time, those behaviors and perspectives that may need to change. For some people it means letting something go and for others to take something on, but it all requires embracing the difficult task of self-reflection and change.

And no one—*no one*—likes change. We generally like change for other people but not for ourselves. Change takes courage, it takes discipline, and it takes hope.

Sounds a lot like Lent.

See it!	Tweet it!	Pray it!

on *STORY*

"It was this Moses whom they rejected when they said, 'Who made you a ruler and a judge?' and whom God now sent as both ruler and liberator through the angel who appeared to him in the bush."

—Acts 7:35

When I feel alone and have lost my way,
God, whisper the stories of those who have come before:
family who has sacrificed much,
friends who have extended love,
and strangers who have been surprisingly present.
Let their stories give form to my own.
Amen.

Some of my fondest memories come from hearing the stories of my grandparents. Stories of growing up in China and the Philippines, making their way to and in the United States, raising kids, going to church, and working in the canneries, fields, and supermarkets filled the ears of my childhood. While certainly time softens the pain and struggles of those stories to the point of being nostalgic, these are the stories upon which my faith has been built.

I can't imagine life or what kind of person I would be if not for the stories of the previous generations.

One of the ways that we can listen for God's calling on our future is by remembering God's movements in the past. Stories told and crafted well give texture to our memories and insight into what we do now. Some stories help us to move through failure and disappointment, while others help us keep perspective about success and achievement. Stories help keep everything in perspective so that we can balance the urgency of today with the knowledge that others have persevered before us.

What are the stories that you have heard? Whose stories do you need to seek out? Of which stories do you need to hear more? Take a moment to listen to and for the stories of yesterday, and God's voice may be heard calling you into tomorrow.

See it!	Tweet it!	Pray it!

on *TIME*

For everything there is a season, and a time for every matter under heaven.

—Ecclesiastes 3:1

God, often my spirit is overwhelmed
by the options, by my schedule,
by the very act of choosing what and when.
Help me to know
when to rest, when to play,
when to ground my feet, and when to walk.
Let my time be aligned with yours.
Amen.

If I were to rewrite this classic passage, my new version would include not only the original lines about life and faith but also such things as:

- a time to nap
- a time to pet the dog
- a time to eat ice cream
- a time to yell at the sky
- a time to let the dishes stay unwashed
- a time to turn the radio up and roll the windows down
- a time to weep for no reason
- a time to thank a teacher
- a time to protest
- a time to sit on the couch and binge watch the *Ghost Whisperer*
- a time to complain about the twitters and "kids these days"
- a time to handwrite thank-you notes because "it would make grandma smile"
- a time to hesitate
- a time to take a chance
- a time to take another nap

What would you add? "A time to _____."

See it!	Tweet it!	Pray it!

on *REVENGE*

Hear a just cause, O LORD; attend to my cry;
  give ear to my prayer from lips free of deceit.
From you let my vindication come;
  let your eyes see the right.

—Psalm 17:1-2

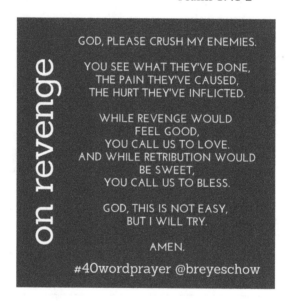

on revenge

GOD, PLEASE CRUSH MY ENEMIES.

YOU SEE WHAT THEY'VE DONE,
THE PAIN THEY'VE CAUSED,
THE HURT THEY'VE INFLICTED.

WHILE REVENGE WOULD
FEEL GOOD,
YOU CALL US TO LOVE.
AND WHILE RETRIBUTION WOULD
BE SWEET,
YOU CALL US TO BLESS.

GOD, THIS IS NOT EASY,
BUT I WILL TRY.

AMEN.

#40wordprayer @breyeschow

God, please crush my enemies.
You see what they've done,
the pain they've caused, the hurt they've inflicted.
While revenge would feel good, you call us to love.
And while retribution would be sweet, you call us to bless.
God, this is not easy, but I will try.
Amen.

Sometimes I wish that I had control of God's [SMITE] button so that every time someone pissed me off, I could zap them off the face of the earth.

When someone cuts me off or won't let me merge when I am driving.

When someone starts a statement with, "I don't mean to be a jerk, but . . ."

When a dog poops on the sidewalk and the owner doesn't clean it up.

When people don't agree with me or won't do what I want them to do.

When people are mean, stupid, or just plain annoying.

Yeah, it's probably good that I don't have access to any gismo or that [SMITE] button that would give me the power to decide who should remain earthbound and who should not. Because like most people, if left up to me and if I had that kind of power, there would soon be few people left anywhere—sometimes an awfully attractive thought but also a very lonely one.

What I need to do is not to respond with like power and retribution but to reframe and remold my responses into ones of graciousness, understanding, and de-escalation. Some may see this as a "kill them with kindness" command or a way to avoid conflict, but I see it as a way not to add more acts of violence and destruction to the world but rather to add to the cause of wholeness, understanding, and care—a much better option for us all.

See it!	Tweet it!	Pray it!

on *LUST*

[T]he Lord knows how to rescue the godly from trial, and to keep the unrighteous under punishment until the day of judgment—especially those who indulge their flesh in depraved lust, and who despise authority.

—2 Peter 2:9–10a

ON LUST #40wordprayer
@breyeschow

When I give in to broken yearnings
that are not of you, O God,
in body, in mind,
in heart, in spirit, or in action,
speak to me in whatever ways that
you must so that I may hear and
embody the healing yearnings you
have for me.

Amen.

When I give in to broken yearnings that are not of you, O God,
in body, in mind, in heart, in spirit, or in action,
speak to me in whatever ways that you must
so that I may hear and embody
the healing yearnings you have for me.
Amen.

Lust is not only about sex.

Oh, you know what I'm talking about. I am not just talking about wanting something real badly but wanting something so much that you are willing to risk anything to get it, to have it, to be with it.

> That new tech gadget you buy even though it is too expensive.
> That ideological fight you enter because you love an online kerfuffle.
> That activity you do knowing it poisons the air and water around us.
> That food you eat knowing that your heart is working too hard already.

No, our lusts are not only about our genital areas being where and doing what they should not be but also about how we engage in behaviors, thoughts, or words that harm and break down relationships. I am the last person who wants to police every moment of our lives, but we do each need to have in place systems to help us discern what is borne out of God's yearnings for us and not solely as a result of our physical reactions, intellectual justifications, and unhealthy socializations.

The battle with lusts will be different for each of us, but with some element of deliberate discernment and acknowledgment, destructive behaviors can be overcome. When addressed well, our relationships, rather than being defined by isolation, brokenness, and pain, can be filled with wholeness, healing, and joy.

See it!	Tweet it!	Pray it!

on *DISTRESS*

In all this Job did not sin or charge God with wrong-doing.

—Job 1:22

ON DISTRESS
#40WORDPRAYER
@BREYESCHOW

God, when I'm in distress
sometimes I just don't understand.
Why me?
What did I do wrong?
Why won't you help?
It is in these times when I struggle
to see you,
to hear you,
to know you.
But I will try to trust you.
Amen.

God, when I'm in distress
sometimes I just don't understand.
Why me?
What did I do wrong?
Why won't you help?
It is in these times when I struggle
to see you, to hear you, to know you.
But I will try to trust you.
Amen.

When something goes wrong in my life, it's so much easier to handle when there is someone who is clearly to blame. It doesn't even have to be someone *else* just as long as I can pinpoint the cause of my discomfort and disruption in life.

I misread the schedule.
The airline lost my bag.
My kids forgot to tell me they need a ride.

When there is a reason, my mind begins to figure out not only how to deal with the current situation but also how to repair any relationships that have been damaged and/or to put in place steps to make sure this doesn't happen again.

But what about those times of distress where the blame is not so easy to place or when there is no logical or reasonable explanation for any of it? It's frustrating, and it reminds us that we do not always know the "whats" and "whys" of life. These are the times when we must simply accept that we don't and won't always know, but yet we must do our best to move forward shrouded in the mystery of God—no easy task.

Distress often generates anxiety and fear, but trust, faith, and hope can guide our way through distress. And if we can rest in these things, we may discover why God has moved in the way God has and discern how to respond to the trials of life, not with distress and anxiety, but with peace and confidence.

See it!	Tweet it!	Pray it!

on *SIGHTS*

I believe that I shall see the goodness of the LORD
in the land of the living.

—Psalm 27:13

AS I LOOK INTO THE WORLD,
I SEE DEATH ALL AROUND ME:
SO MUCH SUFFERING,
SO MUCH DESPAIR,
SO MUCH INJUSTICE,
SO MUCH HATE.
GOD, HELP ME TO SEE THROUGH A
LENS OF LIFE
TO SEE HEALING,
TO SEE HOPE,
TO SEE LIBERATION,
TO KNOW LOVE
AS YOU INTEND.
AMEN.
ON SIGHTS
#40WORDPRAYER
@BREYESCHOW

As I look into the world, I see death all around me:
so much suffering, so much despair,
so much injustice, so much hate.
God, help me to see through a lens of life
to see healing, to see hope,
to see liberation, to know love
as you intend.
Amen.

There are days when I regret reading the paper, skimming my Twitter feed, or listening to the radio. With every report and in every area of human life, there seems to be more and more violence, environmental disasters, misery, hurt, pain, etc.

At times, when I hit a critical mass of the world's struggles, I want to start running down the street with my fingers planted firmly in my ears and singing my favorite 80s' tune at the top of my lungs. Yes, blocking everything out might protect me from the bad stuff. And yes, we all need to take a break, to retreat, and to re-energize our souls. But whether tuning out or taking a break, we can't do so at the expense of seeing the beautiful alternatives that are all around us.

Scandal, murder, and destruction may grab the headlines, but God's events of beauty fill in the cracks. Maybe beauty becomes profound and complex only once we actually allow ourselves to encounter and see it. However, that doesn't change the fact that God's beauty is all around us if we will only take the time to observe the world and not let others dictate our vision of the world.

So yes, we must acknowledge and grapple with human agony, institutional injustice, and environmental destruction; but as we do so, let's remove our fingers from our ears so that we can better observe the subtle and overwhelming ways that God lines our pathways in the world with acts of healing, beauty, and wholeness.

See it!	Tweet it!	Pray it!

on *IMITATION*

Brothers and sisters, join in imitating me,
and observe those who live according
to the example you have in us.

—Philippians 3:17

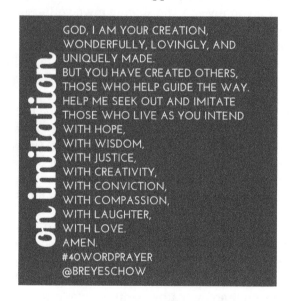

God, I am your creation, wonderfully, lovingly, and uniquely made.
But you have created others, those who help guide the way.
Help me seek out and imitate those who live as you intend
with hope, with wisdom, with justice,
with creativity, with conviction, with compassion,
with laughter, with love.
Amen.

If I had a quarter for every time I was asked, "Is your home-work finished?" or "Did you do your chores?" or "Why are there mashed potatoes on the ceiling?" I would be rich!

Wait, what, no flying tater questions for the rest of you? Oh well, a story for another book.

Never fear, I was also asked, "What do you want to be when you grow up?" and "Who do you admire?" I have always been intrigued by that second question. I think it's an important one, not so that we can live up to misplaced expectations but because one of the ways that we can learn how to be good human beings is by watching others be good human beings—and then doing as they do. My grandfather, who had a tender heart and loving soul; my grandmother, who lived with passionate determination; mentors, who asked the right questions; colleagues, who exuded generous spirits; and the list of those worthy of imitation goes on and on.

While imitation can be the highest form of flattery, it can also be the ways we perpetuate the best of human expression in the world. I know that I am formed by those who model God's hopes in the world. I am impacted by them and do my best to blatantly copy what they do. This is not about wor-shiping others, but seeing them as angels of sorts, imperfect vessels of God's hopes and intentions for the world.

Take a look around you. Who do you imitate?

See it!	Tweet it!	Pray it!

on *WORRY*

How often have I desired to gather your children together
as a hen gathers her brood under her wings, and you were
not willing!

—Matthew 23:37b

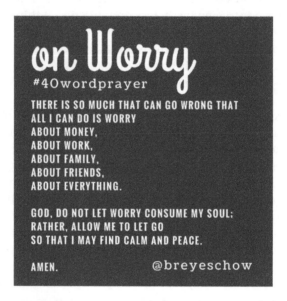

There is so much that can go wrong that all I can do is worry
about money, about work, about family,
about friends, about everything.
God, do not let worry consume my soul;
rather, allow me to let go
so that I may find calm and peace.
Amen.

Our family has recently gone through the college application process.

It was excruciating.

I know that not everyone, either by circumstance or by choice, engages in the college application process, but for those who have, you know what it's like: physically exhausting, emotionally humbling, and anxiety inducing. To be fair, it's a process that is grounded in hard work, hope for the possibilities, and excitement about the future, but it can still feel just awful. The hyped-up expectations, the massive amounts of money, and the false sense of worth that is communicated—all of these things temper anything positive in the process.

The worst part for us, however, was the waiting. To what schools would she get accepted? How much financial aid will we be offered? Which is the best choice? At various times during the waiting process, we had to remind ourselves that no matter how much we worried about the outcome, the decisions were made, the letters mailed, and our fretting would have no impact on the news headed our way. Did that stop any of us from worrying? Nope, but it did help us to laugh at ourselves.

In our worry we can miss out on ways to actually find calm in the midst of wild times, misdirecting our energy away from things that we can change. So we must temper our worry. Easier said than done, but you know what—don't worry about it.

See it!	Tweet it!	Pray it!

on *FAITH*

For if Abraham was justified by works,
he has something to boast about,
but not before God.

—Romans 4:2

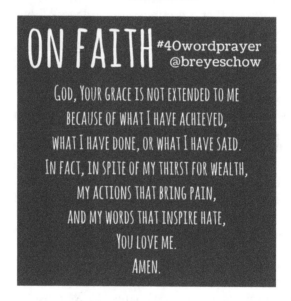

ON FAITH #40wordprayer @breyeschow

GOD, YOUR GRACE IS NOT EXTENDED TO ME
BECAUSE OF WHAT I HAVE ACHIEVED,
WHAT I HAVE DONE, OR WHAT I HAVE SAID.
IN FACT, IN SPITE OF MY THIRST FOR WEALTH,
MY ACTIONS THAT BRING PAIN,
AND MY WORDS THAT INSPIRE HATE,
YOU LOVE ME.
AMEN.

God, your grace is not extended to me
because of what I have achieved,
what I have done, or what I have said.
In fact, in spite of my thirst for wealth,
my actions that bring pain, and my words that inspire hate,
you love me.
Amen.

My wife and I are often complimented because our kids say "please" and "thank-you." I am not really sure what we have done to instill this habit in our offspring. But hey, even if it is blatant public sucking up to the parentals, we'll take it.

One of the things that we do tell them is that they should be respectful in their language even if others are not. I have seen too many people who use manners and being polite as a form of relational currency, expecting others to be polite simply because they have been. I have seen adults act extremely condescending toward young people when it comes to manners. In an attempt to teach manners, before they themselves extend hospitality some adults demand to hear "the magic word" as if to say, "I, the adult, will only be polite to you, if you, the child, are polite to me first." One of these days I would love to hear some kid respond with, "Is the magic word, 'older person who doesn't understand the theological concept of unearned grace'?"

If I could hear it just once, then my life would be complete.

Too often we do unto others the exact opposite of what we are promised by God: love, grace, and presence regardless of what is offered in return. While we should not remain in unhealthy or destructive relationships, we cannot fall into the trap that relationships are based on a currency of behavior. In the end, we must do our best to extend grace, love, and presence freely—even without a "please" or a "thank-you."

See it!	Tweet it!	Pray it!

on *MIRACLES*

Remember the wonderful works God has done,
God's miracles, and the judgments God uttered.

—Psalm 105:5 alt.

on miracles

MY VIEW OF THE WORLD IS BLURRED
BY VIOLENCE,
BY HUNGER,
BY POVERTY,
BY EXCLUSION,
BY HATRED.
GOD, WHEN I FORGET THAT THIS IS NOT WHAT
YOU HOPE FOR THE WORLD,
LET YOUR WORKS COME CRASHING INTO VIEW:
YOUR BEAUTY,
YOUR PEACE,
YOUR COMFORT,
YOUR JUSTICE,
YOUR LOVE.
AMEN.
#40wordprayer @breyeschow

My view of the world is blurred
by violence, by hunger, by poverty, by exclusion, by hatred.
God, when I forget that this is not what you hope for the world,
let your works come crashing into view:
your beauty, your peace, your comfort, your justice,
your love.
Amen.

Whether by reading the paper, listening to the news, or reading social network feeds, it is not hard to see why we humans shouldn't be allowed to have nice things.

You name it, we somehow find a way to mess it up—blatant disregard of the impact of our actions on the environment, our inability to treat human beings with dignity, our failure to adequately support educational systems, our ignorance of institutional racism and sexism that continues to perpetuate marginalization, and the list goes on and on and on.

And yet, despite the vast examples of how badly we can mess things up, miracles abound. We can all point to the person who made it "despite all odds." We are shocked by those times when communities make decisions that eventually make a difference. My mouth drops open when people treat one another with respect and dignity when I least expect it.

Whew, I think to myself, the world is not lost. We have seen goodness.

We must embody the miracles around us and allow them to fuel our hope for what may be if we remain diligent in our work. So let's hold the miracles around us, but not just hold them as a kind of centerpiece upon which we gaze but as a reminder and challenge to make these miracles less miraculous—to make them the norm for us all.

See it!	Tweet it!	Pray it!

on *DOORS*

"When once the owner of the house has got up and shut the door, and you begin to stand outside and to knock at the door, saying, 'Lord, open to us,' then in reply he will say to you, 'I do not know where you come from.'"

—Luke 13:25

WHEN WE SHUT THE DOOR
ON THOSE WHO SEEK ENTRY,
GOD, FORGIVE US.
WHEN WE FAIL
TO RECOGNIZE STRANGER AS KIN,
GOD, FORGIVE US.
WHEN WE KEEP PEOPLE IN THE COLD WHO
NEED TO KNOW WARMTH,
GOD, FORGIVE US.
GOD, FORGIVE US AND MAKE US ANEW.
AMEN.

ON DOORS
#40WORDPRAYER
@BREYESCHOW

When we shut the door on those who seek entry,
God, forgive us.
When we fail to recognize stranger as kin,
God, forgive us.
When we keep people in the cold who need to know warmth,
God, forgive us.
God, forgive us and make us anew.
Amen.

I once had a chess teacher.

He wasn't always my chess teacher.

For the longest time, he was the homeless guy by the door.

And one day he became David, my chess teacher—but only after I opened the door, invited him in, and he came on in.

Metaphorical and actual doors keep us apart every day. Sometimes we are the ones who close, slam, or lock the door, and at other times, we are the ones left standing on the other side, yearning to come in from the storm.

David was one of those standing on the other side of the door, and I kept walking past and closing the door behind me. I was never dismissive, and he was never pushy. We simply never took the chance to cross the threshold together—not until he offered to teach me how to play chess. From that point on, while I was a lost cause when it came to chess, we found a mutual joy in one another's company. And for a brief moment along our individual journeys, we were just two guys sitting at a table, drinking coffee, swapping stories, and sharing grace.

These are the holy moments in life that we miss out on when we fixate on the doors that protect and exclude. Yes, there can be risk. If we are to become the radically diverse household of God, we must open doors and walk right in.

See it!	Tweet it!	Pray it!

on *PURPOSE*

So I have looked upon you in the sanctuary,
beholding your power and glory.

—Psalm 63:2

ON PURPOSE
#40WORDPRAYER
@BREYESCHOW

God, I feel lost.
I am wandering.
I am searching.
Help me to find meaning,
to know purpose,
to find belonging,
and to hear a calling.
And let none of these things be driven by
my wants or needs
but by your hopes and intentions for me.
Amen.

God, I feel lost.
I am wandering. I am searching.
Help me to find meaning,
to know purpose, to find belonging, and to hear a calling.
And let none of these things be driven by my wants or needs
but by your hopes and intentions for me.
Amen.

I know that it will never happen. But if a verified letter from God arrived on my doorstep containing precise instructions for my life, I would not complain. Heck, I would even take a retired messenger pigeon landing on my head with a note that read, "Dear Bruce: You are heading in the right direction! —Love, G."

The search for purpose, meaning, and calling is a lifelong endeavor. During some seasons of life, we may feel on point with our life decisions. At other times, we will understand all too well what it means to wander in a desert. In the end, all we can do is continually find ways to listen for God's guidance, prodding, and challenges.

I have found that, in order to be confident about my current path, I must listen for God in three ways:

1. listening for God's guidance in the stillness and quiet with my mind calm and distractions removed from view;
2. listening to those who know me well, knowing these folks have seen me at my best and worst and can offer reflection on the entire arc of my ministry; and
3. listening to new people who can honestly reflect on current endeavors and remain unaffected by past experiences.

Most folks have the ability to find quiet and connect with people around them. Opportunities for stillness and community simply need to be sought out and committed to. And while this will not guarantee that verified letter from God, it could lessen our need to watch the mailbox hoping that one is on its way.

See it!	Tweet it!	Pray it!

on *LISTENING*

Let anyone who has an ear listen to what the Spirit is saying
to the churches.

—Revelation 3:6

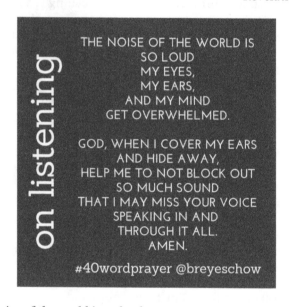

THE NOISE OF THE WORLD IS
SO LOUD
MY EYES,
MY EARS,
AND MY MIND
GET OVERWHELMED.

GOD, WHEN I COVER MY EARS
AND HIDE AWAY,
HELP ME TO NOT BLOCK OUT
SO MUCH SOUND
THAT I MAY MISS YOUR VOICE
SPEAKING IN AND
THROUGH IT ALL.
AMEN.

#40wordprayer @breyeschow

The noise of the world is so loud
my eyes, my ears, and my mind
get overwhelmed.
God, when I cover my ears and hide away,
help me to not block out so much sound
that I may miss your voice speaking in and through it all.
Amen.

"Sorry, mom, I didn't hear you!" was a common refrain from my voice as a child. In fact, if you listen closely enough, you just might occasionally hear me saying the same to my spouse and my children today. Some call this selective hearing, but I prefer to call it discerned listening.

While I am not advocating blatantly ignoring your loved ones, there is something to being able to discern what should or should not be listened to. After all, in a world filled with as much noise as our world is today, being able to figure out what and who should or should not be listened to is important. We can certainly avoid being overwhelmed by the voices by completely blocking out all input from the world, but then we risk missing out on what may be vital. We can miss out on the surprising and subtle ways that God may be speaking to us.

While God may sometimes speak to us with bold clarity, I think God generally speaks to us with nuance and from unexpected voices. With this in mind, we must practice taking it all in and discerning what voices need to be lifted up and amplified for the ears of others as well as our own.

Listening for God is not an easy task. From time to time, we're sure to mishear, ignore, or listen to the wrong voices. This should not, however, deter us from keeping our ears open, for we never know when, where, and through whom God may speak.

See it!	Tweet it!	Pray it!

on *JUSTICE*

[God] expected justice,
    but saw bloodshed;
righteousness,
    but heard a cry!
        —Isaiah 5:7b alt.

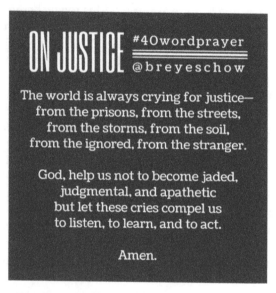

ON JUSTICE #40wordprayer @breyeschow

The world is always crying for justice—
from the prisons, from the streets,
from the storms, from the soil,
from the ignored, from the stranger.

God, help us not to become jaded,
judgmental, and apathetic
but let these cries compel us
to listen, to learn, and to act.

Amen.

The world is always crying for justice—
from the prisons, from the streets, from the storms,
from the soil, from the ignored, from the stranger.
God, help us not to become jaded, judgmental, and apathetic
but let these cries compel us
to listen, to learn, and to act.
Amen.

Being part of the struggle against injustice is in my bones. My grandparents were part of California Central Valley farm worker strikes in the 1950s; my mother raised me to always think about the marginalized as I engaged in politics; my lifelong church, the Presbyterian Church (U.S.A.), at its finest moments, has been part of movements of justice throughout the generations.

But justice work is hard.

It's easy to become jaded and pessimistic. Justice "wins" occur so infrequently that cries of injustice become deafening and overwhelming because they are screaming from all corners of the world. It can just be plain tiring to always be thinking about the impact of our actions and the ways we may contribute to injustices of the world.

Again, justice work is hard.

But as so many have said to me over the years, "No one has ever said faith is easy," and when it comes to a faith that calls one to a posture of justice-seeking, this is evident. Seeking justice means not only fighting for justice in communities and corporations but also fighting the injustices in ourselves—never fun.

So I try to remember that God does remain faithful in the struggle. Despite the hard work and difficulties, I can't imagine that God will ever ask us to stop trying, no matter how hard it is.

See it!	Tweet it!	Pray it!

on *ISOLATION*

I was silent and still;
   I held my peace to no avail;
my distress grew worse,
    my heart became hot within me.
                  —Psalm 39:2–3a

on isolation

BEING ALONE IS NOT ALWAYS LONELY
BUT FOR THOSE TIMES WHEN THE ISOLATION IS REAL,
GOD, MAKE YOURSELF KNOWN
IN A STRANGER'S ACT OF KINDNESS,
IN A FRIEND'S WORD OF PRESENCE,
IN MY COMMUNITY'S OFFER OF HOSPITALITY,
AND IN THE PROMISE OF YOUR STEADFAST LOVE.
AMEN.
#40WORDPRAYER
@BREYESCHOW

Being alone is not always lonely
but for those times when the isolation is real,
God, make yourself known
in a stranger's act of kindness,
in a friend's word of presence,
in my community's offer of hospitality,
and in the promise of your steadfast love.
Amen.

Being alone versus being lonely. I never really understood that idea until I started to nurture my introverted side.

As a public person, some people are surprised to find out that I even have an introverted side. I am not a huge introvert as compared to some of my family and friends, but because of my outward and outgoing personality, people are shocked when I pull away and take time for myself. I have been accused of being aloof because I am not out socializing. Folks have worried about me because I am alone. And I have disappointed people by not being more of the life of the party.

But there are also times when I do feel isolated. People can be around or not, and somehow I have still felt disconnected. Be it something I was going through emotionally, the work situation in which I found myself, or just one of those funks that we can each go through, I have experienced loneliness and isolation.

It is during these times when I covet friends reaching out to connect, family bugging me to be engaged, and God poking at me to look up and see community around me. Sometimes it takes all my energy to step out and reconnect with folks, but I have found, time after time, that when I do—when I allow God to reconnect me with the communities of which I am a part—I am isolated and lonely no longer.

See it!	Tweet it!	Pray it!

on *JUDGMENT*

[A]ccording to my gospel,
God, through Jesus Christ,
will judge the secret thoughts of all.
                              —Romans 2:16

on judgment

AS I GO THROUGH THE DAY, I JUDGE.
SOMETIMES I EXERCISE WISDOM,
EMPATHY, AND GOOD JUDGMENT.
OTHER TIMES I INFLICT ARROGANCE,
CYNICISM, AND CONDESCENSION.
GOD, KEEP MY GOOD JUDGMENT FROM
BECOMING DESTRUCTIVE JUDGMENT.
AND REMIND ME THAT ULTIMATE
JUDGMENT BELONGS TO YOU
AND ONLY YOU.
AMEN.

#40wordprayer @breyeschow

As I go through the day, I judge.
Sometimes I exercise wisdom, empathy, and good judgment.
Other times I inflict arrogance, cynicism, and condescension.
God, keep my good judgment from becoming destructive judgment.
And remind me that ultimate judgment belongs to you
and only you.
Amen.

Sometimes I shock myself by the ways in which I judge other people.

I can whittle them down to small compact boxes of gender, dress, color, geography, shoe choice, hairstyle, laptop selection, and so on. Then, I find myself making all kinds of assumptions about who that person is as a person and place them in some kind of human ranking of worth, value, and status.

This is me being judgmental.

And then there are those times when I am navigating a space, taking in conversation, interacting with people, absorbing the cultural cues, factoring in contexts of geography, age, gender, and more. I help to connect folks who might find some shared values, I invite people into new spaces in order to expand our collective worldview, and I build relationships with folks who are genuinely interesting and intriguing individuals.

This is me exercising good judgment.

Being judgmental is easy. It is often built on fear of the unknown, and eventually it breaks down community. Having good judgment is difficult. It takes time and attention, but it ultimately builds up community. Seeing what goes on in all aspects of society, I fear that we are much more inclined to be judgmental than to have good judgment, and I lament those times when I participate in the tearing down and not the building up.

Clearly, I need to do more of the latter and less of the former. We all do.

See it!	Tweet it!	Pray it!

on *CYNICISM*

And they told him, "We came to the land to which
   you sent us;
it flows with milk and honey, and this is its fruit."

—Numbers 13:27

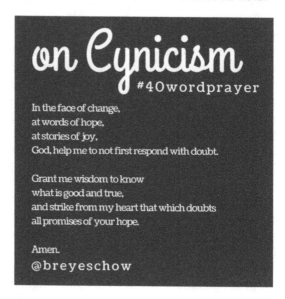

In the face of change,
at words of hope, at stories of joy,
God, help me to not first respond with doubt.
Grant me wisdom to know what is good and true,
and strike from my heart that which doubts all promises of your
   hope.
Amen.

Two of my favorite Muppet Show characters are Statler and Waldorf, the two old guys who sit in the balcony and heckle the rest of the Muppets. Every jab is pointed at how bad the show has been, how bad the show is now, and certainly how bad the show will be in the future. Statler and Waldorf epitomize what it means to be cynical, jaded, and pessimistic.

At times, when I am sitting in a meeting listening to someone lament about how awful things are, all I can picture is Statler and Waldorf. Sure there are times when unbridled optimism can take over, but for people of the Christian variety, too often we forget that ultimately we are a people of the resurrection and hope for what may be and not a people who stay in the death assuming what will not.

Over time, it is easy to fall into a pattern of cynicism. People let us down, expectations are not fully met, and movements of hope seem not to take hold. Sometimes, no matter how hard we try, we are left disappointed.

Truth is, we must not give into or become the Waldorfs and Statlers of the world. Yes, what we expect and hope may not always turn out the way we planned, but that does not mean that our work is without worth. Sometimes, without even knowing it, what looks like failure from the balcony is a whopping success from backstage. But if we give into the Waldorfs and Statlers of world, we will never know.

See it!	Tweet it!	Pray it!

on *NEWNESS*

Happy are those whose transgression is forgiven,
  whose sin is covered.

Happy are those to whom the LORD imputes no iniquity,
  and in whose spirit there is no deceit.

—Psalm 32:1–2

SOMETIMES I NEED
A CLEAN SLATE,
A FRESH START,
A NEW BEGINNING,
NEW LIFE FROM A WORLD
OF DEATH.
GOD, LET ME EMBRACE
YOUR FORGIVENESS
SO THAT I MAY KNOW TO
THE DEPTHS OF MY SOUL
THAT AS I OFFER MY
BROKENNESS
I AM MADE NEW.
AMEN.

on newness

#40wordprayer @breyeschow

Sometimes I need a clean slate,
a fresh start, a new beginning,
new life from a world of death.
God, let me embrace your forgiveness
so that I may know to the depths of my soul
that as I offer my brokenness I am made new.
Amen.

Ask my family. I love to purge.

Like a well-coordinated army unit, you will often hear messages of "Watch out, Dad's cleaning!" being communicated from person to person through our apartment. I admit that I may get a little carried away, but if it has been left out for a significant period of time, it is in danger of being tossed into the donation pile.

When it comes to my surroundings, you see, I love having a clean slate. Every once in a while, my stuff becomes messy, things break down, and my surroundings distract from my work. I am sure some of you have already diagnosed my affliction, but truth is, occasionally clearing the slate is a good thing.

I feel the same way about my life of faith, both the good and the bad. We must sometimes allow ourselves to see things fresh, to let go of old ways of being, and to start over. Of course, I am not talking about the pillars and pylons of faith, only the trappings and distractions that have accumulated around them. After all, when I purge our home, it's the knickknacks, not the refrigerator, that get tossed.

What is given away will be different for everyone. Some will toss burdensome regrets, others will discard mistimed projects, and others will give up practices that have run their course. Whatever we choose to let go, allowing ourselves to reboot and start with a clean slate can be a way to reconnect with God. Happy purging!

See it!	Tweet it!	Pray it!

on *MINDS*

For if we are beside ourselves, it is for God;
if we are in our right mind, it is for you.

—2 Corinthians 5:13

ON MINDS #40wordprayer @breyeschow

PEOPLE THINK WE ARE OUT OF OUR MINDS.
WE LOOK INTO THE EYES
OF THOSE PASSED ON THE STREET.
WE SEE THE HUMANITY OF OUR GREATEST ENEMY.
WE MARCH. WE PROTEST. WE LOVE.
GOD, WE ARE NOT OUT OF OUR MINDS,
BUT OUR MINDS ARE RIGHT WITH YOU.
AMEN.

People think we are out of our minds.
We look into the eyes of those passed on the street.
We see the humanity of our greatest enemy.
We march. We protest. We love.
God, we are not out of our minds,
but our minds are right with you.
Amen.

If God hasn't asked you to do something a little crazy, then you're not listening.

Humans by nature crave safety and security. Security and safety may look different from person to person and community to community, but most of us rarely seek out dangers that truly threaten our security. Some things that my family has done may appear risky, bold, and a little crazy, but rarely do we leave things to chance. We do our research, we do our best to ensure safety nets, and we have a pretty good idea what the outcome will be. Sometimes we undertake these things as a response to God's calling; other times, we simply want to do them, called or not.

Rarely have I taken a true risk to follow God without some sense of certainty and safety. Like most folks, even when we do hear God speaking and calling, we allow the world to convince us why we should choose the rational and sensible path. And when folks are able to step into the unknown, they are barraged with accusations of fanaticism, going too far, acting foolish, and, yes, being "crazy."

At some point we will be asked to step out on faith and trust that God's calling and promise to be with us is true. Easy for God to ask, but harder for us to answer with yes. Someday, I hope to be strong enough to join the ranks of crazy and foolish for God. Until then I will celebrate those who, despite the rest of us saying that they should not, have said, "Yes" to the crazy of God.

See it!	Tweet it!	Pray it!

on *CHOICE*

Turn from your fierce wrath;
change your mind
and do not bring disaster on your people.

—Exodus 32:12b

ON CHOICE
#40WORDPRAYER
@BREYESCHOW

God, when we see wrong,
help us to choose right.
When injustice demands silence,
let me speak.
When violence seeks apathy,
let me act.
When busyness produces chaos,
let me find peace.
For you guide us
and you give us strength
to boldly stand, speak, and act.
Amen.

God, when we see wrong, help us to choose right.
When injustice demands silence, let me speak.
When violence seeks apathy, let me act.
When busyness produces chaos, let me find peace.
For you guide us and you give us strength
to boldly stand, speak, and act.
Amen.

"Make good choices."

This phrase, uttered by my mother since the beginning of time, is being passed down to her grandchildren as we love our own kids into the world.

While met with an eye roll or two, I utter this phrase to my own kids because of the depths of its meaning. For how we choose to live our lives, from the mundane to the momentous, impacts our lives, the lives of our neighbors, and the world. This is not to say that we are all powerful and that we can determine outcomes with a wave of our hand or a word from our mouths, only that there are few neutral actions in the world. With the gift of choice, each of us has the power, ability, and, yes, choice, to act in ways that either build up or tear down.

When I say to my kids "Make good choices," my hopes are that they are kind when indifference would be easier, that they stand up for justice when injustice is faced, that they use their privilege so that others may know harmony and peace, and that they find relationships that will help them grow into who God intends them to be.

These are the hopes that I have, not only for my own kids, but for all children, neighbors, friends, family, strangers, and enemies. For if we all make better choices, we all reap the benefits of a community built up and not torn apart.

Make good choices.

See it!	Tweet it!	Pray it!

on *HYPERBOLE*

God looks down from heaven on humankind
    to see if there are any who are wise,
    who seek after God.

They have all fallen away, they are all alike perverse;
    there is no one who does good,
    no, not one.

—Psalm 53:2–3

IN MY WORST MOMENTS, I KNOW
NO ONE LOVES ME,
EVERYONE IS AGAINST ME,
AND THERE IS NOT A PERSON WHO
WILL CARE FOR ME.
THE EXAGGERATIONS BORN OUT OF
OUR DEEPEST PAIN
ARE EQUALED ONLY BY THE COMFORT
BORN OUT OF YOUR LOVE.
AMEN.

ON HYPERBOLE
#40WORDPRAYER
@BREYESCHOW

In my worst moments, I KNOW
no one loves me,
everyone is against me,
and there is not a person who will care for me.
The exaggerations born out of our deepest pain
are equaled only by the comfort born out of your love.
Amen.

"Don't exaggerate" is about the least effective thing you can say to someone in the throes of a passionate rant or emotional outburst, unless, of course, your objective is to add to the anxiety, aggravation, or anger. After all, it is probably during these times when the *last* thing that will help to bring calm, peace, and some sense of equilibrium is to be told, "Stop expressing what you are feeling!"

There is a place for hyperbole and exaggeration in life. While we can't allow these things to drive relationships, legislation, or public policy, we can appreciate this kind of expression for what it is and what it does—a powerful expression of emotion and a signal to the rest of us of the depth of passion with which that emotion is felt.

While hyperbole can be expressed during times of jubilation and celebration, it is in times of loneliness and struggle when we must be particularly in tune with ourselves and others. Statements about utter lostness, suffering, or isolation can be honest outbursts of emotion. Yet when we begin to believe that those words determine our reality, we must find ways to let the other words seep in that communicate otherwise.

In order to avoid spiraling into an abyss of despair for ourselves or those we love, we must walk the fine line of when to let someone simply be and when to butt in to remind them that no matter how bad things may be today, there is always the possibility for change to come and peace to be felt tomorrow.

See it!	Tweet it!	Pray it!

on *CHEATING*

You shall not cheat one another,
but you shall fear your God;
for I am the LORD your God.

—Leviticus 25:17

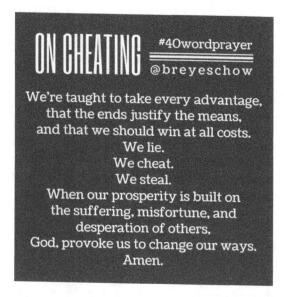

We're taught to take every advantage,
that the ends justify the means, and that we should win at all
    costs.
We lie. We cheat. We steal.
When our prosperity is built
on the suffering, misfortune, and desperation of others,
God, provoke us to change our ways.
Amen.

Each of my children has had to be taught not to cheat.

While "original sin" isn't a fundamental part of my theology, I find it interesting how often I have had to teach kids that cheating is not OK. Somehow they get it into their heads that winning is the goal, no matter what.

Maybe society teaches that cheating is OK—well not maybe, we do. We're taught that cheating in order to win is OK, that the rules apply only to other people, and that the ends justify the means. If the referee doesn't catch you, you didn't commit a foul; if you don't get pulled over, you weren't really speeding; if you can convince someone to make a deal that is bad for them, it's their choice.

The realities of cheating are most evident when people are taken advantage of during times of economic vulnerability. Predatory lending, modern-day indentured servitude, and unlivable wages are all results of people and corporations taking advantage of the desperate circumstances in which many find themselves. And while this may seem victimless and capitalistic in nature, these practices create wealth and prosperity built on the lives of the poor, disenfranchised, and vulnerable.

We may not teach kids to cheat at birth, but we do very little to convince them that it's wrong as they grow up. Maybe we all need another reminder. Don't cheat.

See it!	Tweet it!	Pray it!

on *FORGETTING*

Elisha said to her, "What shall I do for you? Tell me, what do you have in the house?" She answered, "Your servant has nothing in the house, except a jar of oil."

—2 Kings 4:2

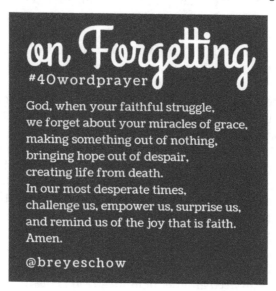

God, when your faithful struggle,
we forget about your miracles of grace,
making something out of nothing,
bringing hope out of despair,
creating life from death.
In our most desperate times,
challenge us, empower us, surprise us,
and remind us of the joy that is faith.
Amen.

Not often enough I go back to my hometown of Stockton, California, and visit my now 80+ grandmother. After my parents divorced when I was still a tot, her house was where I spent much of my childhood. Grandma and Grandpa's home was a place of grounding. Whenever I visit, the memories that come flooding back through the ordinary things always overwhelm my senses:

The cuckoo clock in the kitchen that grandma winds up before bed each night.

The set of glasses collected from some gas station promotion.

The picture collages dedicated to each wedding in the family.

The 1950 record player and radio combo unit that is as big as a couch.

The egg holders that my grandfather and I would use every morning: glass of milk, bowl of Life cereal, and a soft-boiled egg.

The stove in the garage where Grandma would be cooking up a feast.

The mahjong tiles used so lovingly and loudly by our family over the years.

The water kettle, the silverware, and on and on.

Even when I don't need to remember, these are my reminders of the love and hope that have always been present. When I tend to lose sight of God's constancy and grounding, all I need to do is to do the same—look around for the ordinary in life and remember that God has been and will always be here.

See it!	Tweet it!	Pray it!

on *LAUGHTER*

Then our mouth was filled with laughter,
  and our tongue with shouts of joy;
then it was said among the nations,
  "The LORD has done great things for them."

—Psalm 126:2

GOD, THIS DAY WE REJOICE,
WE SHOUT, WE LAUGH:
LAUGHTER BROUGHT ABOUT
BY PLAY,
LAUGHTER BROUGHT ON BY JOY,
AND LAUGHTER BROUGHT ON
BY SURPRISE.
SOUNDS OF LAUGHTER GIVE
DEPTH AND TEXTURE TO LIFE,
SO LET US EMBRACE THE SOURCE
FROM WHICH IT COMES:
YOU.
AMEN.
#40WORDPRAYER
@BREYESCHOW

God, this day we rejoice, we shout, we laugh:
laughter brought about by play,
laughter brought on by joy,
and laughter brought on by surprise.
Sounds of laughter give depth and texture to life,
so let us embrace the source from which it comes:
you.
Amen.

There is nothing more life-giving than to hear the deep belly laugh of a child. There is a sense of utter abandon and unbridled joy that few actions can express like a young child laughing, especially when the laughter is brought on by their unbridled imagination of a nonsensical knock-knock joke.

While many people may use humor as a way to avoid dealing with emotional, personal, and uncomfortable situations, well-timed humor can often break tension, create community, and provoke change. But the humor of children has always been a little bit different. It is humor that is based off of the world around them, a world often not recognized by the adults around them who have constructed a worldview that is static, well maintained, and comfortable. When children tell jokes that make absolutely no sense to the hearer but have the kid doubled over in laughter, I think that is God speaking and laughing the Spirit into the world and letting us know that laughter is a faithful, meaningful, and healing response to both the mysterious and ordinary.

Laughter and humor appear throughout Scripture and are inspired by a variety of things. Sometimes laughter is joyous, sometimes laughter is a response to discomfort, and at other times humor is used to make a statement. So as a child freely laughs at both expected and unexpected events in life, we too need to laugh more, laugh with abandon, and laugh with joy. Knock, knock . . .

See it!	Tweet it!	Pray it!

on *POWER*

I am God, and also henceforth I am God;
there is no one who can deliver from my hand;
I work and who can hinder it?

—Isaiah 43:13 alt.

on power

GOD, WE HAVE A WARPED VIEW
OF YOUR POWER.
WE BELIEVE POWER IS ONLY
ABOUT STRENGTH.
WE HOPE THAT POWER IS USED
AGAINST OUR ENEMIES.
WE CLAIM YOUR POWER AS OUR OWN.
HELP US TO REIMAGINE YOUR POWER:
POWER AS LIBERATION,
POWER AS FREEDOM,
POWER AS CREATION.
AMEN.

#40wordprayer @breyeschow

God, we have a warped view of your power.
We believe power is only about strength.
We hope that power is used against our enemies.
We claim your power as our own.
Help us to reimagine your power:
power as liberation, power as freedom, power as creation.
Amen.

We have a warped and one-sided view of power. It seems that we can only understand power these days by engaging in a contest of physical strength, watching competitors rise to the top, or celebrating the destruction of our enemy. God's power lies not in these things but in how we go about changing the world. Sure, brute force as strength are expressed in God's work, but so is extending healing to the afflicted so that they may find relief, showing love to one's enemy so that they may know God's blessings, and speaking words of insight so that structures of injustice may crumble.

I have always felt this skewed view of power has no long-term value. At some point, organizations and individuals find themselves overcome by weakness. There are always people on the horizon who are stronger and faster and will exert their will on those who find themselves in a state of weakness.

But graciousness, kindness, and empathy never grow old. Graciousness can disarm one's worst enemy. Kindness can transform the hardest of hearts. Empathy can build unexpected bonds of understanding. Faith and the actions generated from them—graciousness, kindness, and empathy—do not weaken over time, no matter our age, physical strength, or weapons stockpile. At the end of the day, love is the most powerful act of faith that we can wield when we go into the world.

See it!	Tweet it!	Pray it!

on *SECURITY*

"If we let him go on like this, everyone will believe in him,
and the Romans will come and destroy both our holy place
and our nation."

—John 11:48

GOD, WE LIVE WITH
SUSPICION.
WE BUILD WALLS,
WE LOCK DOORS,
WE HUNKER DOWN,
WE HOARD OUR RESOURCES,
WE LIVE IN FEAR.
IN OUR YEARNING FOR
SAFETY AND SECURITY,
REMIND US THAT YOU CALL
US TO GO OUT INTO THE
WORLD
AND NOT TO PROTECT
OURSELVES FROM IT.
AMEN.
#40wordprayer @breyeschow

on security

God, we live with suspicion.
We build walls, we lock doors,
we hunker down, we hoard our resources,
we live in fear.
In our yearning for safety and security,
remind us that you call us to go out into the world
and not to protect ourselves from it.
Amen.

We live in a culture of fear.

We hear this all the time. If you keep up with current events, we find ample evidence to support living a life behind tall walls, locked doors, and armed guards. Truth is, unless you're a target of the paparazzi or in an actual war zone, we overestimate the danger of others in order to justify maintaining separation, safety, and security.

Too often we act as if there is danger lurking around every corner. Our stuff can be stolen at any moment. Everyone is working some kind of scam. Sure, these things happen and we need to be wise in our interaction, but if we default to the idea that the world is essentially out to get us, we run the danger of setting up barriers that ensure that we will never really be connected to the world—at least not a world that can expand our understanding of the breadth and depth of God's created and creation.

We cannot be naive. We must do all that we can to fight the urge to put up physical, institutional, and spiritual walls that keep safe and known people in and dangerous and unknown people out. When we refuse to give in to the dangers that the world inspires and we cease our fixation on security, we do away with the fear that drives the building of those walls in the first place and we disassemble the barriers between the reality we choose to claim and the truth that God may hope for us to know.

See it!	Tweet it!	Pray it!

on *DISAGREEMENT*

And let us consider how to provoke one another to love and good deeds.

—Hebrews 10:24

WHEN MY FAMILY CAUSES FRUSTRATION;
MY FRIENDS, EXASPERATION;
LEADERS, DISTRUST;
AND STRANGERS, DISDAIN;
GOD, HELP ME NOT TO RESPOND SO THAT
CONFLICT AND DIVISION INCREASE
BUT TO ANSWER WITH CARE AND
GRACIOUSNESS
SO THAT WE MAY GROW INTO WHOM YOU
HOPE AND INTEND US TO BECOME.
AMEN.

ON DISAGREEMENT
#40WORDPRAYER
@BREYESCHOW

When my family causes frustration;
my friends, exasperation;
leaders, distrust;
and strangers, disdain;
God, help me not to respond so that conflict and division increase
but to answer with care and graciousness
so that we may grow into whom you hope and intend us to
become.
Amen.

When I talk with folks about the Internet, one of their constant struggles and critiques is that it allows people to be nasty and mean to one another. I am not talking about trolls and keyboard commandos who see their life's aim is to find and attack anyone who holds a differing view. I am talking about your friends, family, colleagues, and acquaintances with whom you disagree about important things and who make you to want to throw your laptop out the window in the hopes that it lands on them.

There are a few ways to respond to online nastiness. The easy route is to remove them from view by "unfriending" or "unfollowing" them. It's incredibly satisfying to send a passive-aggressive zinger. Or, scorching them by dropping f-bomb-laced air raids of comments that question their intellect and ability to walk and chew gum at the same time, which feels really good, at least for a moment.

PRO-TIP: when it comes to the third option, [Backspace] is your friend.

I truly believe that the best response is to stick around and engage. When it makes sense, interact; when things get heated, be a witness to a different way of being; and in the in-between times, build the relationship by participation in the wonderfully ordinary times of life. You have some connections with these folks. If there is *ever* going to be a change of heart in them or you, connections must be maintained, thirsts for vanquishing denied, and disagreeing in new ways lived.

See it!	Tweet it!	Pray it!

on *HUMILITY*

"The trees once went out
   to anoint a king over themselves.
So they said to the olive tree,
   'Reign over us.'"

—Judges 9:8

ON HUMILITY
#40WORDPRAYER
@BREYESCHOW
When I don't know everything,
the wise guide me.
When I can't do everything,
hands support me.
When I can't get through anything,
communities care for me.
God, remind me that when I don't
always know the way,
through the acts of others
you make the way known.
Amen.

When I don't know everything, the wise guide me.
When I can't do everything, hands support me.
When I can't get through anything, communities care for me.
God, remind me that when I don't always know the way,
through the acts of others
you make the way known.
Amen.

When I was in elementary school, I had a fight with my uncle, who was helping me with my math. The entire episode ended with me crying, screaming, throwing my book on the floor, and hiding under my bed.

At the time I must have felt that he was a domineering math ogre. As I got to know him as an adult, I can't imagine that he was anything but calm and understanding. In fact, he must have been chuckling at the whole thing.

But, dammit, I was right—except that I wasn't.

I would like to think I've learned to regulate myself a bit more since then, but I can assure you that, on more than one occasion, the movie playing in my mind during some disagreements often ended with me running away and hiding under the bed.

Because dammit, I am right—unless I am not.

In later years my uncle and I laughed about that day. While I was clearly wrong, I was young, so the laughter was all the apology needed. As adults, we are often unwilling to admit that we don't always know the answers. Even when we are made aware that we might have been mistaken, apologies are hard. At the end of the day, if we are to grow in mind and spirit, we must seek and accept help, and when we are wrong, admit it.

It beats hiding under the bed.

See it!	Tweet it!	Pray it!

on *MERCY*

O LORD, I have heard of your renown,
    and I stand in awe, O LORD, of your work.

In our own time revive it;
    in our own time make it known;
    in wrath may you remember mercy.

                      —Habakkuk 3:2

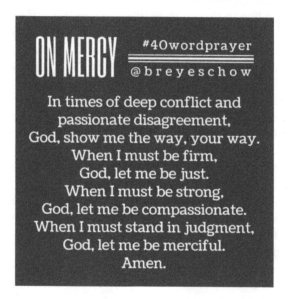

ON MERCY   #40wordprayer

@breyeschow

In times of deep conflict and
passionate disagreement,
God, show me the way, your way.
When I must be firm,
God, let me be just.
When I must be strong,
God, let me be compassionate.
When I must stand in judgment,
God, let me be merciful.
Amen.

In times of deep conflict and passionate disagreement,
God, show me the way, your way.
When I must be firm, God, let me be just.
When I must be strong, God, let me be compassionate.
When I must stand in judgment, God, let me be merciful.
Amen.

I have always been struck by how some believe that showing mercy is a sign of cowardice and weakness when in fact it is a sign of confidence and strength.

Thanks to the movies, we generally think of mercy during times when someone has the power to determine life or death for someone else. It's purely physical, and it's always held in tension with the idea that showing mercy equals weakness.

Mercy can be different than that, both in its situation and in its meaning. Mercy can also be called for in times when power is held over someone in workplace hierarchies, in housing placement, in family systems, in educational systems, and in our penal system. Mercy is not about right or wrong or if someone deserves punishment but about how power is wielded by those who have it. To offer mercy is not about offering absolution or erasing the past but offering an alternative response to domination and control. In fact, those who choose mercy show more confidence, as it shows security of self and the ability to have compassion in the face of defiance and conflict. They who have power also have the sole responsibility to extend mercy or not.

Choosing revenge and retribution is to walk a path paved by insecurity and fear, whereas to choose mercy is choosing a road paved with confidence and compassion. In our individual and collective lives, may we choose a path of mercy.

See it!	Tweet it!	Pray it!

on *GRIEF*

Be gracious to me, O LORD, for I am in distress;
   my eye wastes away from grief,
   my soul and body also.

                               —Psalm 31:9

ON GRIEF #40wordprayer @breyeschow

MY HEART HURTS BEYOND WORDS.
MY BODY SHEDS TEAR UPON TEAR.
MY SOUL CRIES OUT IN PAIN.
GOD, HELP ME NOT TO RUSH MY GRIEF;
LET ME HOLD IT AS LONG AS I NEED
AND LET IT BE LOOSED WHEN THE TIME IS RIGHT.
AMEN.

My heart hurts beyond words.
My body sheds tear upon tear.
My soul cries out in pain.
God, help me not to rush my grief;
let me hold it as long as I need
and let it be loosed when the time is right.
Amen.

We are uncomfortable with sadness and grief.

Sure, we can deal for a short while, but as soon as a person's grief makes us feel uncomfortable or becomes inconvenient, we want the sadness to end and for people to "move on" as quickly as possible so that the rest of us can too. Most of the time these hopes are well-intentioned. However, when it comes right down to it, society does not make much room for people to grieve in the various ways as they need.

Because we see grief as a problem to be fixed, we don't allow people to move at their own pace. We try to force people through stages. We project our own process or discomfort onto others. We forget that we all grieve in different ways. Sometimes, we simply need to give someone room to do so.

Grieving for as long as one needs can be cathartic in the long run. We must not allow ourselves to sink into the places that lead us to self-destruction. Sitting with sadness and loss for as long as we need can make us whole on the other side of grief.

So sit with your grief and allow others to do the same. The time to move on will make itself known when and how God intends. When we do so, our moments of grief, filled with loss and sadness, may be reborn as a life filled with abundance and joy.

See it!	Tweet it!	Pray it!

on *EMPATHY*

Because he himself was tested by what he suffered,
he is able to help those who are being tested.

—Hebrews 2:18

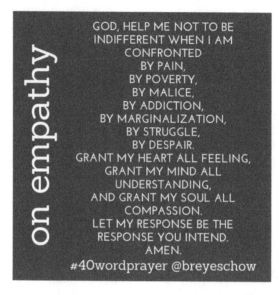

GOD, HELP ME NOT TO BE
INDIFFERENT WHEN I AM
CONFRONTED
BY PAIN,
BY POVERTY,
BY MALICE,
BY ADDICTION,
BY MARGINALIZATION,
BY STRUGGLE,
BY DESPAIR.
GRANT MY HEART ALL FEELING,
GRANT MY MIND ALL
UNDERSTANDING,
AND GRANT MY SOUL ALL
COMPASSION.
LET MY RESPONSE BE THE
RESPONSE YOU INTEND.
AMEN.
#40wordprayer @breyeschow

*God, help me not to be indifferent when I am confronted
by pain, by poverty, by malice, by addiction,
by marginalization, by struggle, by despair.
Grant my heart all feeling,
grant my mind all understanding,
and grant my soul all compassion.
Let my response be the response you intend.
Amen.*

"Empathy // [em-puh-thee] —noun. [T]he psychological identification with or vicarious experiencing of the feelings, thoughts, or attitudes of another."*

In the face of struggle, conflict, and pain it is one thing to understand or to sympathize, but it is quite another to have empathy. Sure, our minds can grasp the realities of the situation, and our hearts can communicate our sadness. Yet when our souls are shaken out of a deeper connection, we want none of that.

The hardest part about being empathetic is that it requires us to feel that which we do not want to feel. The natural reaction is to try and distance ourselves from those feelings, to intellectualize issues, and to strip the human element away from the situation. While some distance may be healthy and helpful, it often leaves those who are suffering without support to help alleviate and address the cause of their suffering.

In the face of struggle, we must embrace empathy as a powerful gift and not see it as an excuse to create distance. The more empathetic that we are with one another, the more that we can find common ground with one another. And when we, as individuals, experience commonality, in both celebration and struggle, we are more apt to positively address suffering—together, with heart, mind, and feeling.

See it!	Tweet it!	Pray it!

* http://dictionary.reference.com/browse/empathy

on *REST*

Six days shall work be done; but the seventh day is a sabbath of complete rest, a holy convocation; you shall do no work: it is a sabbath to the LORD throughout your settlements.

—Leviticus 23:3

ON REST #40wordprayer
@breyeschow

God, I am so tired.
Tired of the competition to be the best,
tired of the comparisons
between everyone,
tired of the constant need to be busy.
Tired. Tired. Tired.
God, in your presence,
let me rest my soul,
rest without guilt,
rest without productivity.
Rest. Rest. Rest.
Amen.

God, I am so tired. Tired of the competition to be the best,
tired of the comparisons between everyone,
tired of the constant need to be busy.
Tired. Tired. Tired.
God, in your presence, let me rest my soul,
rest without guilt, rest without productivity.
Rest. Rest. Rest.
Amen.

I love a good power nap.

In the car during my kids' soccer practice, on the couch with a puppy curled up on my lap, or on the floor of my office in between meetings, the power nap is symbolic of what I must keep reminding myself to do in my life—take time to rest.

I realize that not everyone has perfected the art of the power nap or simply doesn't want to try. Some have never been able to sleep in short intervals, others think naps are a waste of time, and others have never given lunchtime naps a second thought since kindergarten naps were forever taken away.

I have found that, whether it be a nap at the end of a series of interactions, a day off at the end of some frenzied days, or a vacation after a season of busyness, it is vital for us all to carve out time to rest, rejuvenate, and recreate before the next season of activity. If we do not, we will soon find minds, bodies, and spirits that are burned out and our relationships with ourselves, others, and God to be in disarray.

So whatever and however you grab your seventh day after six days of work, be sure to take that day, make it holy, and allow yourself to be renewed. Just as God answered the call for rest after so much creativity and creation, so too must we.

Good luck and good rest—I'll be over here taking a nap.

See it!	Tweet it!	Pray it!

on *ANIMALS*

Your righteousness is like the mighty mountains,
   your judgments are like the great deep;
   you save humans and animals alike, O LORD.

—Psalm 36:6

God, we live as if human life is the only life.
Just as you have cared for humans and animals,
let humanity do the same.
Let us tend to all creatures:
the cute, the cuddly, the majestic, and the peculiar.
For you have created us all.
Amen.

We have the cutest dog.

I declare this with all the bluster and confidence of parents who also proclaim that they have *the* cutest children—*we have three of those also*—but, seriously, we do.

Someday, we are going to find out that dogs actually understand us and love us anyway, which would make them even more amazing—but I digress.

Let's be honest, not all animals are cute.

Our family has a saying whenever we see a creature that falls to the bottom of the cute basket: "It is still a creature of God." While we say this mostly to remind us that the creepy crawlies of the world are important, it does act as a reminder that God cares for all creatures of the earth, and we should as well.

Whether it be the environmental impact of development, the humane treatment of animals in the food industry, or the place of domesticated animals in urban life, too often it seems that we create situations where a humans versus the animals posture takes hold. I wonder if that always has to be the case, that someone has to win and the other lose?

If we each allowed our understanding of animals—cute and creepy alike—to expand, I suspect that we might find solutions where neither humans nor animals have to lose, but both are in a sense safe, respected, and given life.

See it!	Tweet it!	Pray it!

on *DOUBT*

"While you have the light, believe in the light,
so that you may become children of light."
After Jesus had said this, he departed and hid from them.

—John 12:36

ON DOUBT #40wordprayer @breyeschow

GOD, WHEN I AM STRUGGLING
TO FEEL YOUR PRESENCE,
PLEASE MAKE YOURSELF KNOWN.
WHEN I NEED SILENCE IN ORDER TO LISTEN,
GRANT ME SILENCE.
WHEN I NEED WORDS IN ORDER TO SPEAK,
GRANT ME WISDOM.
WHEN I NEED COURAGE IN ORDER TO ACT,
GRANT ME CONVICTION.
AMEN.

God, when I am struggling to feel your presence,
please make yourself known.
When I need silence in order to listen, grant me silence.
When I need words in order to speak, grant me wisdom.
When I need courage in order to act, grant me conviction.
Amen.

I often hear people say, "Doubt is a part of faith."

While I agree with the intent of the statement to address the difficulty and discomfort many have with reconciling doubt and faith, I also know that doubt sucks and that getting to the point of being comfortable letting doubt and faith dance together can be a long haul.

As I have wrestled with this over the years, I have found myself looking often for signs that God is somehow showing up in the world. I don't see this in sporting events or award shows—*I don't think Jesus actually cares much about these things*—but I do try to take a moment and watch the world a bit more carefully than I might otherwise: stopping to take in the stunning beauty of things that I might otherwise pass by, claiming love that is extended to me by my spouse that might otherwise be taken for granted, and noticing miracles of individual or corporate movement that might otherwise go unnoticed. Making sure that I do these things helps to temper my doubt.

I try to allow the pockets of doubt that exist to give fullness to my faith. Doubt compels me to seek and know God's truth more than I would otherwise, and it serves as a reminder that we are never truly done growing in faith.

And for that doubt, I am grateful that it is part of my faith.

See it!	Tweet it!	Pray it!

on *LEARNING*

GOD has given me
    the tongue of a teacher,
that I may know how to sustain
    the weary with a word.
Morning by morning he wakens—
    wakens my ear
        to listen as those who are taught.
                —Isaiah 50:4

on learning

DON'T WORRY, GOD,
I HAVE IT ALL UNDER
CONTROL,
I KNOW WHAT I'M DOING,
I'M DONE LEARNING, AND
I DON'T NEED TO LISTEN.
DO I?
GOD, HELP ME TO BE MORE
TEACHABLE TODAY
THAN I WAS YESTERDAY
AND TO BE MORE
TEACHABLE TOMORROW
THAN I AM TODAY.
AMEN.

Don't worry, God,
I have it all under control, I know what I'm doing,
I'm done learning, and I don't need to listen.
Do I?
God, help me to be more teachable today than I was yesterday
and to be more teachable tomorrow than I am today.
Amen.

About ten years ago I was talking with one of my mentors about ministry. I asked him why he didn't say anything to me during *one* of the epic failures that I engineered early in my ministry.

He responded, "You weren't teachable."

Well then.

He was basically saying, "Yeah, you were too arrogant to listen and learn—you big jerk." I added the "jerk" part—*but, knowing this mentor, he might have used even more colorful language*. He was right. At that point in my life and ministry, I was not willing to listen, learn, and change.

I choose to believe that I am better today. There are still times when I find it difficult to admit that I may need help. Somewhere deep down, I still feel that asking for and receiving help somehow communicate weakness and are detrimental to my work. Intellectually, I understand the opposite to be true. Seeking and accepting guidance only strengthen what I do and are signs of confidence and security. I am not always driven by my intellect. Shocker. Sometimes, I just don't want help.

So the journey continues. I am still at times unteachable, but I am striving to be more open today than I was yesterday and more open tomorrow than today.

See it!	Tweet it!	Pray it!

on *GRATITUDE*

Maundy Thursday

What shall I return to God for all God's bounty to me?
—Psalm 116:12 alt.

GOD, WHY SHOULD WE DO WHAT WE DO?
LIVE HUMBLY SO OTHERS WILL BE
HUMBLE?
SEEK JUSTICE SO OTHERS WILL BE JUST?
SHOW KINDNESS SO OTHERS WILL BE
KIND?
NO, WE ARE . . .
HUMBLE, BECAUSE YOU'VE LIVED HUMBLY;
JUST, BECAUSE YOU'VE SHOWN JUSTICE;
KIND, BECAUSE YOU'VE BEEN KIND.
AMEN.

ON GRATITUDE
#40WORDPRAYER
@BREYESCHOW

God, why should we do what we do?
Live humbly so others will be humble?
Seek justice so others will be just?
Show kindness so others will be kind?
No, we are . . .
humble, because you've lived humbly;
just, because you've shown justice;
kind, because you've been kind.
Amen.

There are always places in life where pain and hurt reside. If we look hard enough, we can also name much for which we can be grateful. For some, joy may be found in a family that provides support and perspective; for others, purpose may be known in work that is grounded in a deep calling; for others, conviction may be fueled by physical health and the wonder that is breath.

But so what?

Being thankful is not the end of our journey of gratitude. Our gratitude must translate into a life of service to others. If we fail to live our thankfulness outside of ourselves, we become hoarders of grace, which is no way to show gratitude and no way to live thankfully.

On Maundy Thursday and the remembrance of Jesus' washing of the disciples' feet, we see what it means to let loose lives of service fueled by gratitude. When feet are washed, naked clothed, hungry fed, ignored seen, outcast embraced, and unloved loved, we live gratitude in a way that honors the many gifts in our lives. In this holy act of giving away and serving, we avoid hoarding life-giving moments, and we do so not with resentment or fear but with joy and thanksgiving.

So, as you gather around the table, break bread, and serve one another, do so fully embodied and freely given with life, thanksgiving, and joy.

See it!	Tweet it!	Pray it!

on *JUSTIFICATION*

Good Friday

> Then he handed him over to them to be crucified.
>
> —John 19:16

ON JUSTIFICATION
#40WORDPRAYER
@BREYESCHOW

The injustices of the the world can be
overwhelming,
so we turn away,
we walk away,
we give in.
God, in the face of injustice, give us
humility to see our involvement,
courage to step in the way,
and faith to trust your power
over others.
Amen.

The injustices of the world can be overwhelming,
so we turn away, we walk away, we give in.
God, in the face of injustice, give us
humility to see our involvement,
courage to step in the way,
and faith to trust your power over others.
Amen.

Good Friday, the day we remember the death of Christ, is for me the most moving service in the church year. Remembering the depths of pain that humans can cause one another is vital. In a culture that jumps too quickly to the positive spin, the good story, and the fairy-tale ending, the Good Friday reminder of death gives depth to moments of joy. To fully appreciate the power of the resurrection, new life out of death, and hope out of despair, we must walk the depths of death and despair.

We have such a difficult time embracing our role in death: the walk to the cross, the preparation for death, and the striking of nails. Like we do with many difficult aspects of the faith story, be it the filth of the manger, the rape of Bathsheba by David, or people being massacred in the name of God, we make these things palatable by sanitizing, justifying, or simply turning the page.

We, in essence, explain away the worst of our faith story so that we can move on to the best. When we do this, we give ourselves permission to do the same when it comes to today. When it comes to people living in poverty, sexualized and raped, or murdered on the streets, we sanitize, intellectualize, justify, or simply walk right on by.

So, we pause on this day of death to remember. In doing so, we give ourselves the chance to be a part of a lifetime of hope.

See it!	Tweet it!	Pray it!

on *DESPAIR*

If mortals die, will they live again?
   All the days of my service I would wait
   until my release should come.

—Job 14:14

on despair

· ·

IT HURTS.
MY BODY. MY HEART. MY SOUL.
GOD'S GENTLE WHISPERS REMIND ME
THAT HOPE
WILL DELIVER ME FROM DESPAIR
AND FROM DEATH,
NEW LIFE WILL BE KNOWN.
I HAVE SEEN IT, I HAVE KNOWN IT,
AND I HAVE LIVED IT.
BUT TODAY, I YEARN FOR HOPE LIKE
NEVER BEFORE.
AMEN.

#40wordprayer @breyeschow

It hurts. My body. My heart. My soul.
God's gentle whispers remind me
that hope will deliver me from despair
and from death, new life will be known.
I have seen it, I have known it, and I have lived it.
But today, I yearn for hope like never before.
Amen.

I am not sure that I have ever known real despair.

I have experienced excruciating physical pain, I have felt deep emotional sadness, and I have wandered the realms of spiritual isolation. I have seen despair in the eyes of those close to me, and I have tried to comfort those filled with it. Despair has always been woven throughout the lives of those whom I have pastored, but I have not known despair in its most crushing and desolating form.

When someone near to us is in such pain, what is there to say? What do you say to a parent when their child has died? What do you say to someone when her brother is murdered? What do you say when cancer is found too late to treat? Some responses are trite, cliché, and ultimately useless. When folks want to know why something has happened, we try to give an answer, to explain the pain away, to give false hope—even as we are just as confused, angry, and struck as everyone else.

I have found that the best thing to do is simply to remain at a wail's distance. Just in case you are needed to comfort, to offer sustenance, or to witness a miracle, you will be present. Just as many waited around the body and tomb of Jesus, sometimes we are called to wait, hope, and pray that despair, in God's time, will be transformed into hope.

See it!	Tweet it!	Pray it!

CONCLUSION

We made it.

If you used this book as your Lenten discipline, Happy Easter and a hearty "Alleluia! Christ is risen!" to you. If you simply used a prayer or two for you or your community, thanks. However you used these prayers, I am grateful.

As I reflect on the process of writing *40 Days, 40 Prayers, 40 Words*, I already miss the discipline: wrestling with Scripture, crafting words, and articulating meaning. As any writer, preacher, or teacher should, I have been changed by the process of creating this work. I deeply appreciate your picking this book and sharing a little part of your spiritual life with me. Your support allows me to keep learning, stretching, and growing in my own faith as I hope some of these words have helped you to grow in yours.

I am always curious about how folks will experience words that I share and whether my hopes and intentions will come through. At the same time, I also understand that any creative contribution to the world will provoke different reactions from each person. So whatever your particular reactions have been, I will trust that which was helpful, comforting, or provoking was known and whatever missed the mark or simply didn't connect with you will float away until another day.

I would love to get your feedback, know how you used these prayers, or just connect as common travelers on the journey. So please feel free to connect with me via the "keep in touch" section, and I will do my best to respond. Thanks again for spending a few moments with me in prayer, and peace be with you.

KEEP IN TOUCH

I genuinely enjoy connecting with people on various social networks, so please feel free to keep in touch. While I don't promise to respond to each and every connection, I will do my best to do so. I can be found via @breyeschow on 99.967 percent of most social networks. As of today, here is where you can find me most of the time.

- **Website** [www.reyes-chow.com]: Current blog, bio, contact info, and more
- **Mailing List** [http://madmimi.com/signups/29509/join]: Sporadic but fun
- **Facebook Page** [www.facebook.com/breyeschow]: Here I curate links and conversations about race, faith, parenting, gun violence, design, sexuality, politics—pretty much anything that I find useful, interesting, or inspiring.
- **Twitter** [https://twitter.com/breyeschow]: Fair warning, I tweet 10–14 times a day, sharing a mix of personal whimsy, current events, and curated political content. Twitter is where I interact with folks the most, and I can be found via @breyeschow.
- **Instagram** [https://instagram.com/breyeschow]: Instagram is my happy place. I love seeing people's lives as viewed through their eyes. I generally post about my travels, my kids, my very cute dog, and, yes, my most scrumptious meals.
- **Instapray** [www.instapray.com]: In addition to the prayers from this book, I post prayers here about once a week. There is a broad theological spectrum that I often find surprisingly moving. This is an app, and I can be found at @breyeschow.

See you around the Interwebs!

RESOURCES

For those of you who would like to try this at home, here is the list of resources that I used in creating this book. Dive in and have fun!

- **Oremus Online Bible** [http://bible.oremus.org]: A free online Bible resource.
- **Google Drive** [https://www.google.com/drive/]: Drive is a great collaboration tool and was used to hold and share all documents and images.
- **Google Docs** [www.google.com/docs/about]: The original manuscript was written entirely using Docs, although other software was used for editing and publishing.
- **Google Shortener** [https://goo.gl]: Shortener was used to generate shortened URLs and all Quick Read (QR) Codes.
- **Canva** [www.canva.com]: Canva, an online image-creation site, was used to create the prayer graphics. Canva will change your life. Seriously.
- **Instapray** [www.instapray.com]: All prayers were shared on Instapray. Providing diverse theological views, Instapray is a place to connect with people around the joys and struggles of life. You can access these posts though the "Pay it" link or QR Code. Find me on Instapray via: @breyeschow.
- **Twitter** [https://twitter.com]: All prayers were posted on Twitter and can be retweeted via the "Tweet it!" links. Find on Twitter via: @breyeschow.
- **Website** [www.reyes-chow.com]: My blog is designed using Wordpress [https://wordpress.com/], the domain name is registered on GoDaddy [www.godaddy.com], the

site is hosted on HostMonster [www.hostmonster
.com], and the blog theme (as of April 2015) is DW Fixel
by DesignWall [www.designwall.com/wordpress/themes/
dw-fixel].

You can find referral links and more resources at [www
.reyes-chow.com/referrals].

CPSIA information can be obtained
at www.ICGtesting.com
Printed in the USA
LVHW05s2344110518
576870LV00013B/598/P